THE 21ST OCTOBER 2016 DYN DDOS CYBER-ATTACK ANALYSIS

The Attack That Broke the Internet for a Day

By

Sam El Gbouri

Fellowship for Doctorate in Information Assurance
Masters in Science in Cybersecurity

--- December 9th, 2017 ---

Copyright

Printed in the United States of America via CreateSpace Print on Demand 2018

ISBN-13: 978-1721165230
ISBN-10: 1721165231

El Gbouri, Abdessamad (Sam)
Abdessamad.elgbouri@gmail.com

Dedication

To my Wife Meriem, the smart Loving, caring, best 75% of me, I could say best half but it wouldn't be true she is more.

To my eldest son Elyas, the intelligent artist, the caring, and good-to-mom son

To my youngest son Adam, the strong, the smart, the patient, and loving son

And to my Mother Haddou, the Judge Daughter and politician wife, and more importantly the sacrificing mother, and the five sons protector.

Table of Content

Introduction

Cybersecurity postures and effectiveness of the policies and related procedures in addition to the efficient implementation of controls are the main concerns organizations strive to achieve. However, in some instances challenges may seem harder to overcome with the available solutions and implemented controls. The present work extends on one of the examples of damaging cyber-attacks namely the Dyn Distributed Denial of Service Attack (DDoS), the approaches taken prior and after the attack, recommendations will be presented to strengthen the information security stance of organizations that could be struggling with these types of challenges.

The Attack Analysis: The Approach

York, (October 22, 2016) the chief strategy officer at Dyn provided an official statement a day after a major distributed denial of service (DDoS) cyber-attack. In this statement York revealed that the attack was: "a sophisticated and highly distributed attack involving 10s of millions of IP addresses", he also confirmed that with the help of analysis provided by Flashpoint and Akamai (two cybersecurity professional breach analysis organizations): "the source of the traffic for the attacks were devices infected by the Mirai botnet". In the present section the Dyn DDoS will be analyzed from the details prior the attack, to events and technical information about the attack, to the approaches taken by Dyn about information security or IS assessments and IS solutions plans.
Recommendations on those assessments and plans will be revealed at the end of the section.

Chapter One
Background of the Events

On October 21, the Dyn attack Shocked the internet community because it showed that a well committed and knowledgeable cybercriminal group could cripple the internet infrastructure if they have the right tools and are fueled by an unwavering drive or incentive, a taught too frightening to even think about. The facts remain that the Dyn Attack was not intended against any customer of Dyn but to simply interrupt Dyn's services as reported by Greene (October 21, 2016) executive editor at networkworld.com. To fully understand the event leading up to the attack, it is important to consider the main cybersecurity mediatized events of the weeks leading to the attack. Many considerations should be accounted for in late 2016, from the international geopolitical changes, to the advancements in technology, and abundance of internet access and cybersecurity tools, in the next section a thorough look into the state of the world from multiple perspectives is outlined.

1-1. Timeline of Events Leading Up to the 21 October 2016

The United States computer emergency readiness team or US-CERT is a central hub for reported attacks and vulnerabilities in the United States, they have alerts broadcasted almost daily based on the events and cyber-attacks happening in the world accumulated from reported attacks in the US and partners from all over the world, the following are multiple noteworthy events leading up to the attack on Dyn on the 21st October 2016:

- 14 October 2016: US CERT ALERT (TA16-288A): this alert was published by US-CERT only one week before the attack, and it clearly warns professionals about the danger of the Mirai Botnet, and shared the extent of the attack on two websites, the Brian Krebs security blog on krebsonsecurity.com and a French webhost OVH, where krebsecurity.com may have been targeted by a botnet: "exceeding 620 gigabits per second (Gbps)" (US-CERT Alert TA16-288A), and the French webhost a DDoS attack with at least 1.1 terabits per second (Tbps). To understand the values of these numbers it suffices to understand that a typical network device may have a performance of 10 Gbps as explained by Schudel, (n. d.) a network consulting engineer with Cisco. This means that a 620 Gbps, for example, is way above the traffic a simple network device could handle, therefore the attacked server will naturally deny service even to the legitimate web requests.

- On October 17, 2016: US-CERT reported on Week 3 of cyber security awareness month organized in partnership with the Department of Homeland Security (DHS) and the National Cyber Security Alliance, during this campaign the focus was on increasing cybersecurity awareness and it included: "deleting suspicious communications, being aware of "too good to be true" offers and using strong authentication" (US-CERT Week 3, October 17, 2016).

- During the week of 17 October: US-CERT released bulletin SB16-298 which is the week vulnerability summary, it is a summary of vulnerabilities recorded by the National Institute of Standards and Technology (NIST), the National Vulnerability Database (NVD), the NVD is sponsored by the Department of Homeland Security (DHS), the National Cybersecurity and Communication Integration Center (NCCIC), and the US-CERT. these vulnerabilities are relevant to the present studied attack because they show that Linux vulnerabilities were of the highest risks (US-CERT Bulletin SB16-298, October 24, 2016), especially since the IoT devices part of the Mirai botnets are generally based on Linux Operating Systems, Arrow (September 13, 2016) a global provider of enterprise computing solutions explained that based on a survey conducted with developers of IoT devices over 70 % answered that Linux is the most used in those devices. This shows, in volume, how appealing the Linux OS vulnerabilities are for attackers planning on DDoS attacks.

Coincidentally, US-CERT published the same day of the Dyn Attack a Linux kernel vulnerability known as Dirty COW (CVE-2016-5195), and a recommendation was given to review Linux systems vulnerability databases including the Red Hat CVE database (US-CERT Kernel, October 21, 2016), the Dirty COW can allow an attacker to locally leverage this vulnerability and gain root privileges (US-CERT Vulnerability Note VU#243144, October 21, 2016).

- On October 25, 2016 US-CERT posted about week four of the national cybersecurity awareness month, where it provided a note about a security tip that was previously posted and updated (US-CERT Security Tip ST05-017, October 25, 2016), and the subject of the note was on cybersecurity for electronic devices and gave thorough recommendations for information security protection.

1-2. Socioeconomic State of the World

1-2-a. Demographic and socioeconomic.

The world health organization provided a thorough analysis of the demographic and socioeconomic factors of the world, it showed that countries are seeing more economic growth, and becoming more urbanized, and people are becoming more educated (WHO statistics, 2009). On the other hand, technological advances are gaining speed and countries are continuously changing and facing struggle from every perspective to keep pace with nowadays challenges, as reported by Willige, (2017) from World Economic Forum, Willige also reported in the same source on the Human Capital Report of 2016 (HCR, 2016) that: "rich and poor countries alike are struggling to keep pace with this new era, dubbed by many as the "fourth industrial revolution"

1-2-b. Internet and doing business, reliance and convenience.

In 2010 households with internet access at home were 71.8% and in only 5 years that percentage reached 82.6% of the population, and the telecommunications investment went from 17% of revenue in 2010 to 31.9% of revenue in 2015 per the World Bank Group (2017), these indicators are not specific to the United States alone, based on the World Development Indicators the trend is seen all over the world and even much accentuated in many countries (World Development Indicators, 2016).

These types of usages and investments are indicators of the consumer satisfactions with the internet necessities as well as the requirements businesses found themselves obligated to accommodate, such as more convenience for the consumer, services rendered at a click of a button, and actions and products delivered in record times, things that can make the difference between a lucrative business or a dying one, selling online and providing and delivering services or merchandises as quick as possible has become the ultimate goal for any businesses thriving to utilize the internet to its full extent, making it extremely challenging for those businesses who can't compete.

1-3. Cultural State

1-3-a. Social networking.

In 2012 the daily time spent on social networking by internet users worldwide was reported by statista.com (2017) as 90 minutes per day, and in only 5 years it increased by 45 minutes to reach 135 minutes per day, that is an average daily usage calculated based on worldwide statistics, but it is visibly apparent to the internet community observers that many users in the United States reach way more than 2 hours of social networking a day especially the youth. This presence in the social media provided a new opportunity to many businesses, they use the newly found platforms to advertise products and services, and reach a well-needed audience and potential customers, or they use it to secure direct or indirect sales with a large base of consumers.

1-3-b. A blur of all barriers.

The international statistics presented by the World Development Indicators (2016) showed that education, economic growth, reliance on the internet, inflation, as well as unemployment are all seeing generally positive changes, although more challenging to maintain. The barriers between countries have been blurred, mainly because communication and information about almost anything are attainable via the internet in some way or another.

Other noteworthy considerations are:

- The distance between countries was shortened since it has become easier to travel either because flights are more available or more affordable.
- Languages are no longer a barrier, nowadays users can easily find a wide variety of translation software, and translation mobile applications, in addition to the satisfaction some people find in learning more than one languages causing a new trend in languages learning.
- Technological limitations are no longer a problem for others to compete with the United States. In "The world is flat" best seller book, Friedman (2005) explains that the capabilities of all countries in the world are nowadays the same almost everywhere on the planet, and he shared what he called the ten flatteners to cite only few he mentioned workflow software, uploading, informing, and what he called "the steroids" which are wireless capabilities, voice over IP (VoIP), and file sharing (pp-51-199).

1-4. Technological Advancements

1-4-a. Internet of things.

The internet of things is said about devices that have the capability to connect to the internet but not the same way a user does in a computer, they connect to get updates, to get firmware upgrades, to receive updated useful data for the user, for example a refrigerator that can have updated information on the weather outside and the actual outdoors temperatures, or a baby camera that can show the baby sleeping on a mobile phone screen, or baby playing seen remotely where a mother monitors her baby left with a babysitter. The list of devices is becoming longer by the minute, almost every device in the household has a variation that has IoT capabilities.

1-4-b. Advanced persistent threats.

Advanced persistent threats (APTs) are at the epicenter of any cybersecurity professionals concerns mainly because of the damage it can cause and the challenges they may face when trying to defend against it. Attackers materializing exploitations of these threats utilize a sleuth of highly sophisticated methods and mechanisms, one of those mechanisms is utilizing Botnets such as the Mirai Botnet that crippled the Dyn servers during the October 21, 2016 attack, Thakar and Parekh (2016) provided a thorough study of Botnets as APTs, and they concluded that APT Botnets are: "powerful soft instruments (weapon or crime vehicle) for state-sponsored attackers with scalable computing power to conduct cyber offensive of arranging stealthy cyber espionage campaigns". This conclusion can only be true of the Dyn attack because it was a powerful cyber offense.

1-4-c. Advanced open-source malware engineering and re-engineering.

With the increasing appeal for malware, attackers usually share their codes on hacking websites, and it doesn't take long for any code to be re-engineered and morphed to a new version of a malware, these capabilities have been opted even by the good guys mainly to understand malware and proactively create malware defenses, Malware analysis reverse engineering (MARE) methodology present helpful tools and well-organized process flow to help analysts master their trade, in addition a new timeline was developed called the Malware defense timeline, and it helps map out the research goal to eliminate the malware as explained by Nguyen, and Goldman, (2010).

1-4-d. Hackers have the edge.

Hackers have the edge and defenders are lacking efficient defensive mechanisms. Because defenders are trying to avoid becoming on the wrong side of the law, they are almost always behind in malware reverse engineering, and in timely patching their systems and networks against zero-day threats. Hackers exploit any existing vulnerabilities disregarding the damage it may cause, they test their codes on any vulnerable system and any dropped shell is a success for them (dropping shells is the technical wording for breaching or penetrating a system), where at the opposite side of the spectrum the defenders have to test and retest their solutions and patches before introducing additional vulnerabilities to their systems, which keeps them on edge.

The other plus hackers have is the abundance of hacking tools and harmful malware, it takes only one search session in a search engine for "black hat" and the results will be phenomenal and dangerous websites. At the time of writing these lines a search of this kind revealed many places that will with no doubt have malware injection threats embedded in the websites, so defending in cybersecurity can always come with the price of increased risks to the defender's machines, systems, and networks. Some of the results and websites the above search revealed are "hacking tutorial", "EvilZone", "Hack a day", "hack in the box", "hack this site". As outlined by Dube (2009).

1-4-e. Always online capabilities and increased storage capabilities.

In a paper titled: *"Constantly connected: at what price and with what rewards?", Mark et al.,* (2016) explained that with the increased computer capabilities and the abundance of storage:

> Our lives will be increasingly
> captured lifelong to be part of
> the cyberspace for recall and
> other uses. Therefore, as
> individuals we are approaching
> constant online connectivity,
> given this inevitability, the
> challenge is to recognize the
> hazards of constant connectivity
> and enjoy the benefits (p. 205).

With the increased internet bandwidth internet service providers (ISPs) offer, and the increased online storage, it has become a trend to stay always connected, smartphones are connected 24/7, home computers are always connected to the internet, and only rare users take the time to disconnect from the network when not needing the internet, the challenge is that every internet capable device will need and want to connect either to updates or to run properly. This behavior has become so abundant that many tech giants incorporate the need for always online in many of their devices, Windows 10 for example will want to always connect, and it can't be properly installed until the user provides a user account with Microsoft or other.

1-4-f. Increased computational capabilities.

Not long ago a computer with dual microprocessors and a two Gigabytes of RAM was considered a fast computer, it had just enough computational power to do word processing some graphical processing, some basic gaming, and browsing the internet, with more services and more web application requiring more and more resources computers had to evolve, and as the Bell law said in the theory of the computers' evolution: "a new computer class forms and approximately doubles each decade, establishing a new industry" Bell (2008).

With these new capabilities it is possible for hackers to use brute force attacks, and dictionary attacks to breach many of the poorly protected computer systems, they can infect devices like the IoT devices with malware by simply attacking their basic security and embedding the malware for later deployment or use as a launch platform for DDoS attacks, as it was the case for the Mirai malware in the Dyn attack, Mirai uses a brute force attack with the help of a dictionary attack on IoT devices with only 60 common usernames and passwords like "root" and "admin" or "support" for usernames and easy default passwords like "default" or "123456" or "password", and they were able to assemble an army of botnets that cripple not only Dyn but other tech giants as well as explained by Herzberg, Bekeman, and Zeifman (2016).

1-5. Cybercriminal Behaviors and Earnings Prospects

The world of cybercriminals is an underworld mainly controlled by greed and disregard of the rule of law, especially in countries that haven't fully implemented and enforced laws and regulations against hacking, although the standards are well known and easily adaptable to any country regardless of local languages or cultures. In an article about how much money hackers make, Weissman (2015) from Businessinsider.com reported on findings of a company called Trustwave specialized in infiltrating hacker groups to understand their business models get: "an early look at the malware hackers are cooking up"

This underground is so sophisticated and enclosed unless fully vetted and sponsored by other cybercriminals, the findings reported by Weissman (2015) show where hackers meet and complete their transactions like cybercrime forums, buying and selling fully loaded exploit kits ready to use, distribution of cryptowall defense to generate revenue from ransomware, or sell services to make exploits more successful and malware undetectable by security protective software (called obfuscation services). In the same source, Trustwave calculated how much a hacker could make, it came to $84,000 a month, and most importantly Trustwave reported that: "even non-technical criminals can easily set up a malware campaign and make major revenue" (Weissman, 2015).

1-6. Standards and Policies

Because of the considerable technological advancements, and the spread of cyber threats, and the increasingly challenging task of protecting data and privacy, many organizations have united their efforts to draft more stringent guidance in cybersecurity, and cover whatever information security professionals may forget or omit from their planned information security controls. NIST for example works closely with the federal government to draft the most relevant examples of policies, procedures, and implementations, and ways to test the effectiveness of the implemented controls via risk analysis assessments and enterprise-wide risk assessments (ERM).

Not long-ago information security (IS) was a non-existing department, but nowadays it is a department with the utmost importance, and in many instances, their leaders enjoy the best pay in the organization, they must be part of every major decision making, and they should be consulted with any major planned change. Not only they have to be skilled IT professionals but they have to be versed in forensic analysis and investigative tools in project management, and more importantly they have to be versed in writing information security policies, a matter that not only information security leaders have to be fully invested in but also the organization leadership as well, Barman, (2002) stated in his book *"Writing Information Security Policy"*: "it is not enough to bless the information security program; management must own up to the program by becoming a part of the process." And he explained later that the pretext that management is not trained in IT is not a valid reason and that it is mainly to guarantee that business processes are safeguarded and not hindered by security decisions (p. 27).

1-7. DYN the Domain Name Service Provider

Dyn is a part of the Oracle family as of not long ago, it is a specialized service provider mainly internet intelligence and traffic control, the service about internet intelligence -network enables their customers to: "avoid service interruptions, reduce costs, and deliver the best possible online experience by monitoring and analyzing Internet performance" as stated in their website (Dyn Internet Intelligence, n. d.). The managed DNS on the other hand is a service that they claim can boost performance and reliability of online applications, ensure the most responsive and resilient managed DNS service, and streamline administration with Dyn management portal and logging and reporting tools. In addition, Dyn Claims that their cloud-based service saves their customers time and money since they don't need hardware nor IT professionals to manage it, and most importantly they are advertising that they have the latest DNS technology (DDoS mitigation, IPV6, DNSSEC) (Dyn Managed DNS, n. d.).

Chapter Two
The Dyn DDoS
Attack Details

Much ink was spilled covering this attack, although didn't affect much the common man, it was felt by all giant tech companies, it made it all too real to simply discount it as an acceptable risk, the damage could be of monumental proportions, so many organization went the extra mile trying to fully grasp their infrastructures vulnerabilities, although it is fully understood that absolute solutions can't be implemented and will never prevent all attacks, it is always hopeful that the more an organization information security team knows about these attacks the better they will be prepared mitigating their risks. This chapter will relate some of the technical details on this DDoS attack.

2-1. Overview of the Attack on DYN

York, (October 22, 2016) provided an official statement the next day of the attack, he explained that on Friday October 21 Dyn was the victim of a high scale DDoS attack that affected their East coast first, then West coast. The attack started at 07:00 am ET and if affected mainly the East coast directed traffic, it was mitigated and service was restored, but then another attack started right before noon ET, and it was global affecting all traffic managed by Dyn, service was restored at approximately

1:00 pm ET. A third attack was verified the same day but was mitigated without any customer impact.

2-2. Technical Details on the Attack

Green, (October 21, 2016) an executive editor at networkworld.com outlined the timeline and the details of the attack, he relied on experts in cybersecurity event monitoring such as ThousandEyes a network monitoring service provider and Level 3 a network security service provider part of the CenturyLink family. the attack on Dyn was very organized, and supposedly involved thorough planning, at the level of a sophisticated project management endeavor, it was timely prepared in several phases, East coast, then East and West coasts and then in the evening of October 21, 2016 it went global where at 07 pm ET a second wave hit 20 Dyn data centers around the world, this suggests extensive time management planning was involved, the scope and the goal were clear at this point, the victim is definitely Dyn but not his customers as Green Stated.

The project management body of knowledge (PMBOK guide) 5th Edition explained the main phases of a project they are generally forty-five logically grouped project management processes, but are categorized into five process groups: initiating, planning, executing, monitoring and controlling, and finally closing. The Dyn Attack showed all five processes in play. There was a clear understanding of the scope of the attack: Dyn, then a serious planning was in place since attacks went up in scale and geographical implication from East to West to global, execution was the reason it had this much media coverage even if it was for only one day. The monitoring and controlling phase of the PMBOK show in the form of the continuous fight, although the Network Operations Center at Dyn were fighting back using all their mitigation techniques the attackers kept launching attacks in waves suggesting they are monitoring the responses form Dyn NOCs. The closing phase of the PMBOK is not necessary because the goal is not to close the project and let the victim deal with it. Eventually the attacks ended the same day.

2-3. Mirai Malware, the Weapon of Choice

As explained previously the malware used is Mirai and it allowed the creation of a massive botnet made from IoT devices like baby monitors, home routers, DVRs, and other home devices connected to the internet and with limited security such as devices with default usernames and password. The Mirai source code was apparently posted on the internet as open source making the determination of who really created the malware almost an impossibility. Krebs (January 2017) posted in his online blog what he believed the identity of the maker of Mirai, Supposedly the developer of Mirai is called Anna Senpai, but it was never confirmed by official authorities.

2-4. Building a Mirai-powered Botnet

The easy distribution of the malware is what made the number of infected devices so large, the Symantec Security Response explained (October 27, 2017) some frequently asked questions about the Mirai Malware, especially how it works and what makes it so resilient, they explained that the malware continuously scans for vulnerable devices and infect them, these devices will start reporting to a central command and control server, and may receive commands to pin a target and cause the DDoS attack. The question was: how to remove the Malware? Symantec answered that once the IoT devices are turned off the Malware is removed, but because of the continuous scanning the device may be infected within minutes as soon as it is back online unless the device access codes credentials (username and password) are changed.

The estimated number of devices used to launch the Dyn attack were estimated by Mr. York Dyn Chief Strategy Officer to be in the range of 10s of millions of IP addresses, the attack reached over 600 Gbps. Many other reported attacks using the Mirai Botnet had much higher bandwidth reaching in some instances over 1Terabytes per second (Tbps).

2-5. Launching the Attack

The Mirai malware was identified by Liu (December 9, 2016) from Symantec as a Trojan horse Virus with a low-risk level called Linux.Gafgyt, the author explained the detailed technical process it follows to operate and propagate as shown in figure 1 below:

Discovered: October 2, 2014
Updated: December 9, 2016 4:48:05 PM
Type: Trojan
Systems Affected: Linux

The Trojan searches for routers by reading the following file name:
• /proc/net/route

The Trojan attempts to brute-force the routers using commonly used usernames and passwords.

The Trojan may connect to one of the following servers:
• 162.253.66.76, port 53
• 89.238.150.154, port 5
• 108.162.197.26

The Trojan may accept the following commands from the remote server:
• PING
• GETLOCALIP
• SCANNER
• HOLD
• JUNK
• UDP
• TCP
• KILLATTK
• LOLNOGTFO

The Trojan may steal system information from the following location and send it to a remote server:
• /proc/cpuinfo

Figure 1: Symantec technical information on Mirai

(Linux.Gafgyt). Retrieved from
https://www.symantec.com/security_response/writeup.jsp?
docid=2014-100222-5658-99&tabid=2

As shown above the command Mirai accepts from
the command and control server will dictate the capabilities
that will be possible to achieve using the infected devices,
and they are many, from "ping" for DDoS to Scanner for
propagation, and TCP for transferring data across the
internet to the remote server. Hilton, (October 26, 2016) the
GM and VP, Product Development at Oracle Dyn provided
some details on the attack, and he stated that the traffic was
caused by requests in the form of "TCP and UDP packets,
both with destination port 53 from a large number of source
IP addresses".

Schneier, (November 1, 2016) speculated on an
article published on SecurityIntelligence.com, a partner of
IBM, stated that the reason for the attack was: "probably
not originated by a government. The perpetrators were
most likely hackers mad at Dyn for helping Brian Krebs
identify — and the FBI arrest — two Israeli hackers who
were running a DDoS-for-hire ring.", of course this too was
never officially confirmed as stated by Flashpoint one of
the two official cybersecurity firms that helped Dyn unveil
some of the details on the attack and attackers (Nixon,
Costello, and Wikholm, October 25, 2016).

Chapter Three
The Dyn DDoS
Event Analysis

The last chapter explained some of the simple technicalities exploited by the attackers, but the full technical aspects could be outside of the scope of the present work, as it is extremely technical and requires a deeper understanding of advanced networking and malware engineering, this subject will be further analyzed in one of my future more technical books.

The present chapter however will relate the event and its repercussions on the industry stakeholders, from the end-user, to the employee, and the society and the economy as a whole.

3-1. Extent of the Attack Damages

Reported damages, 1 hours of no connectivity from 07:00 am ET to around 08:00 am ET for all users trying to connect to East Coast websites Dyn provides DNS services to. Another hour from around 12:00 pm ET to 01:00 pm ET but this time with repercussion on the connectivity of Dyn Clients to the West Coast and the rest of the world, the last wave of attacks in the evening was reported to have no impact on the customers because of the implemented mitigation solutions.

Some of the companies affected by the Dyn Attack were, Amazon, Twitter, Tumblr, Reddit, Spotify, and Netflix, it suffices to consider only these few Giants to see the amounts of lost business, especially since they all rely on the e-commerce and the conveniences it provides customers, however Simmons (October 25, 2016) from BitSight.com a security ratings firm, explained some detailed information on the industries most affected, he stated that: "Media and Entertainment businesses were affected the most, followed by Technology." This suggests that the media and entertainment businesses lost a lot more than Amazon losing business for over two hours of inactivity.

Hilton (October 26, 2016), shared the main points learned about the DDoS attack on Dyn, one of the problems was that: "the Attack generated compounding recursive DNS retry traffic, further exacerbating its impact", this means that session connection requests had to retry the requests increasing the traffic and causing more congestions.

Domestic information security ramifications, with an attack of the magnitude of Dyn DDoS attack, the cybersecurity community will have another strong point to do more about cybersecurity, it is fortunate added and needed skill for them but probably unfortunate for the organization because they should invest in cybersecurity solutions that may or may not prevent DDoS attacks like the one that crippled Dyn for the majority of a day. Another aspect of domestic repercussions are the trust companies will have with their DNS service providers, and how can they ensure they have alternative solutions when attacks like these happen, especially because all indications point to the increase of IoT devices numbers and that attacks will only get stronger and more sophisticated.

International information security ramifications, Hilton (October 26, 2016), provided a detailed account and timeline of the attack, he stated that in the morning of the attack the operations support team started noticing elevated bandwidth against Dyn Managed DNS platform in the Asia Pacific, South America, Eastern Europe, and US-West regions, then the East coast was fiercely targeted, then finally targeting all 20 global Dyn Data centers making the attack a historical event as stated by York, (October 22, 2016).

3-2. How did Customers React?

Some customers dropped from the list of Dyn supported clients like PayPal and others, but many stayed like Amazon who backed Dyn, especially because a DDoS is almost inevitable, particularly for organization aggregating risk like Dyn, they are at the front gate of all traffic to be redirected to and from their clients, and much of the challenges come from outside traffic, of course there is mitigation solutions like advising multiple DNS providers, but again, Dyn will never advise a client to have more than one DNS provider because it is not a sound business decision coming from Dyn. Few of the other companies who are reported to be a success story with Dyn are Evernote, Zillow, CNBC, Etsy, Hershey's, Zappos as advertised in the Dyn Website on their customer success stories (Why Dyn, n.d.).

3-3. what does it mean for the society?

End-users don't usually care much about where their internet packets go and how there are routed and who routes them, but they care a lot more about the speed of execution of their messages, shared pictures and files, and more importantly their communications, and access to their platforms. If the internet speed is throttling they will feel it and they may even change their internet service providers, they may opt for different types of hardware, but suffering from the chocking effects of s DDoS attack affecting not only their ISP but also access to their own work websites is a bit more to accept, frustration can build up, unhappiness with their jobs can become debilitating, and unfortunately employees will start losing motivation, and productivity could be seriously hindered, and this is only in the work environment.

In private lives: it is even worse to imagine the effects of no internet access. Nowadays almost every aspect of our lives is managed via a digital footprint, our communications are all digital, and the majority of our tools are based on some digital solution that uses some type of an internet connectivity, and more importantly many solutions are based on the "always online" capabilities, especially monitoring systems that relate real-time status of machines and operations, especially critical operations such as health monitoring machines, and infrastructure monitoring controls, a loss of connectivity in some of these solutions could be life altering.

The Dyn attack suffered only for one day, and it wasn't the doing of a government, so it is easily imaginable that state warfare could very easily be looking at solutions and capabilities of this kind, the STUXNET is only one of them, but what the future hides is even more frightening than could be imagined, although risks could be studied and mitigated, or accepted, the only question is to what level could risk acceptance be considered.

Chapter Four
The Dyn Approach Analysis

4-1. DYN Reactions

Dyn, called now Oracle Dyn, has a DDoS approach published since July 21, 2016 authored by Steadman (July 21, 2016), and is still the article used to explain how Dyn specifically monitors and triages a DDoS attack (para, 1). The exact ways the organization reacted to the attack is not published and not easy to find online, and if it is found it will not always be a trusted source, the hint was clearly given by York (October 22, 2016) when he said: "At this point we know this was a sophisticated, highly distributed attack involving 10s of millions of IP addresses. We are conducting a thorough root cause and forensic analysis, and will report what we know in a responsible fashion" (para, 7), the emphasis should be on the last two words: "responsible fashion", that means it is irresponsible to give more than what should be revealed, and understandably so, telling the attackers how they could mitigate what Dyn mitigated would be ironic and not a good idea, so at this point the approach published July 21, 2016 will have to be accepted at face value as Dyn DDoS approach.

Dyn provided a protection stack summary illustrated in figure 2 below:

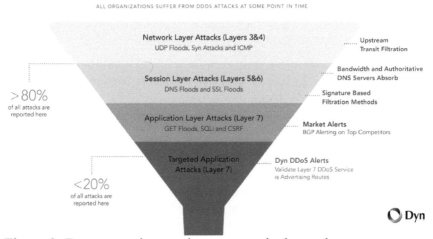

Figure 2: Dyn protection stack summary, it shows the approach being identification, then mitigation, and validation. By Steadman (2016). Retrieved from https://dyn.com/blog/ddos-mitigation-inside-dyns-internet-performance-management-approach/

The explained approach in figure 2 talks about three important phases: identification, mitigation, and validation. The identification's goal is to identify the sources of the DDoS attacks and isolate the traffic or redirect it to other regions of the world, Dyn's approach explained the mean time to identification (MTTI), and they claim that since Dyn operates a global IP Anycast network they ensure workload continuity and decreased MTTI which improves the mean time to mitigation (MTTM), Mohan (2010) supports Dyn Claim about Anycast and explained it thoroughly as follows:

Anycast allows multiple, identical, globally deployed DNS servers to advertise the same IP address. For all intents and purposes, the same server exists in dozens or hundreds of places simultaneously. When an Internet user looks up your domain name, they find the Anycast instance topologically closest to themselves. Usually, there's a correlation between network topology and physical geography.

The last phase in Dyn's Approach about DDoS attacks is: validation, during this process Dyn examines its internet performance management platform and ensures that: (1) Dyn's filters are performing properly (firewall filters), (2) the geographic location of the problem is pinpointed as accurately as possible (to allow authoritative DNS traffic steering and BGP re-routing when needed), (3) the traffic is normal, and (4) Dyn's third-party monitoring is healthy (Steadman, 2016). This latter item could be the most interesting since it provides Dyn with an outsider assessment of its internet performances

Reactions to the attack

One can only speculate on the real reactions of Dyn Stakeholders, the leadership has a planned deal with Oracle to purchase Dyn in only a few weeks from the attack, the employees were expecting great things from this new deal, customers were hoping for probably reduced costs and better options and services, but above all, only the media was really served by this attack, Dyn attack was at the front of all media outlets technical or not. Some sources say that Dyn Lost some 14,000 customers, and it is understandable if they really did, but nowhere to confirm it, the media speculated in all fronts, about who caused the attack, who created the Mirai Malware, who launched the attack, and why, no certain answers so far.

One fact is sure, many actions must have been taken

including restructuration, and thorough enterprise-wide risk management (ERM), policies and procedures revamping, attract more investments with better solutions and explanations as well as ensuring good customer service and increasing customer satisfaction. Work on the human capital, better the workforce morale, and increase their trust in the organization prospects.

4-2. Available Literature on InfoSec Assessments and Solutions Plans by DYN

4-2-a. Short term approach.

Dyn has a full section in their website on DDoS and understandably so, since they provide Managed DNS services, and it has become apparent for cybersecurity observers that DDoS attacks have increased in size and complexity, Dyn provided the following statistics: between 2015 and 2016 the DDoS attacks increased by 71%, the more advanced DDoS attacks called by Dyn the infrastructure layer DDoS attacks increased by 77% and the attacks over 100 Gbps increased by 138% (Dyn DDoS, n. d.).

Sloper, (2016) explained few of the solutions an organization can do to protect itself from DDoS attacks, he gave the following advices:

- Be prepared and aware

- Use tools and install technology promoting the understanding of normal behaviors of the organization's network.

- Inform IT teams of any abnormal incidents (like DDoS attacks), mainly to allow them to take the proper timely remedial actions.

- And finally, the most important solution is to use: "redundant cloud and CDN services together with internet performance management tools with traffic monitoring and rerouting capabilities" which can redirect traffic to alternative non-affected hosts.

4-2-b. Long-term approach.

The closest to what could be considered a long-term approach by Dyn to avoid DDoS attacks is what Steadman (2016) shared about the use of Dyn's internet performance management approach. Especially when he explained the need to properly document incidents to be referred to when needed, he advises the utilization of the impacted business continuity plans and the network incident response plans and updates them with relevant data for future implementations and mitigations. Steadman explained that any newly learned information about an attack such as the specifically targeted protocols and the employed tactics could be added to the information security team playbooks as well as in its forensics standard operating procedures.

4-3. Proposed Alternate InfoSec Assessment and Solution Plan

4-2-a. Short term approach.

Convery, (2012) from CISCO, explained in his detailed book Network Security Architecture that a DDoS attack affects the 3rd and 4th OSI layers, and that it can be detected by intrusion detection systems (IDS) or by log analysis, but he provided some ways of protection against those sophisticated flooding attacks including the implementation of committed access rate (CAR), specific filtering, ISP options (with prior agreements) (p. 98). More detailed technics include the use of Access Control Lists (ACLs) configured throughout an ISP's network, although it is time-consuming and not so effective compared to other techniques such as Black Hole Filtering (routing targeting traffic to "null0" also called the bit bucket) and Sinkhole Routing (routing the traffic towards a honeypot or such for further analysis and tracing-back capabilities) (Convery, 2012).

An organization could limit the damage of a DDoS attack if they isolate the source of the attack and finding its approximate geographic area. To determine that location an ISP can use one of the two main techniques: Manual ACL Trace, or Backscatter DDoS trace back who are basically two clever methods to trace back to the source of the attack.

US-CERT DDoS (2014) provided a quick DDoS guide, it explained the attack possibilities by OSI layer, the possible DDoS traffic types, and more importantly the mitigation of large-scale DoS/DDoS attacks, figure 3 below explain few possible mitigation solutions.

Mitigating Large Scale DoS/DDoS Attacks

Device	Layer	Optimized for	DoS Protections
Firewall	4-7	Flow Inspection, Deep Inspection	Screen, Session Limits, Syn Cookie
Router	3-4	Packet Inspection, Frame Inspection	Line-Rate ACLs, Rate Limits

Some DDoS Mitigation Actions and Hardware

- Stateful inspection firewalls
- Stateful SYN Proxy Mechanisms
- Limiting the number of SYNs per second per IP
- Limiting the number of SYNs per second per destination IP
- Set ICMP flood SCREEN settings (thresholds) in the firewall
- Set UDP flood SCREEN settings (thresholds) in the firewall
- Rate limit routers adjacent to the firewall and network

Figure 3: US-CERT DDoS quick mitigation guide, showing the OSI layers that could be compromised. Retrieved from https://www.us-cert.gov/sites/default/files/publications/DDoS%20Quick%20Guide.pdf

4-2-b. Long-term approach.

Schneier, B. (November 1, 2016) explains what could be learned from the Dyn Attack, and he advised that if needed, an organization can purchase DDoS protection from many companies, but he also confirmed that attacks are possible, and will succeed if large enough, this could be a long term approach where the organization should keep an eye on the trends in cybersecurity and the ratings and capabilities of the company protecting its interest against DDoS attacks, and have contracts that are not too long (2 to 3 years renewable) in order to have the option to change them if needed. Another long-term approach could be to select an ISP who can provide attack mitigation capabilities, like allowing basic ACL, Black Hole Filtering, and Sink Hole Routing, in addition to manual ACL Trace Back and Backscatter DDoS TraceBack.

The attack on Dyn was the biggest and most sophisticated attack, gave the impression it was thoroughly planned, and its execution was timely and laser-focused on each of the planned milestones, first the east, then the west, and finally the world. This type of attacks used botnets that are increasing in number strength by the minute, meaning the future attack can only be wider and larger, and more sophisticated, and unfortunately more effective, the only best plan for an internet infrastructure to stay safe from it is to prepare for it with back-up solutions and be ready to involve the ISP and all its partners to overcome the challenges ahead because the question is no longer: could an attack that can cripple the internet for longer period of time happen? But rather: when? And could an organization recover from it? This scenario will be revealed in my next book: *The Internet Collapse and the Next Society. Technological, Societal and Economical Analysis.*

∞∞∞

Chapter Five
The Author Take

The attack on Dyn was the biggest and most sophisticated attack, gave the impression it was thoroughly planned, and its execution was timely and laser-focused on each of the planned milestones, first the east, then the west, and finally the world. This type of attacks used botnets that are increasing in number strength by the minute, meaning the future attack can only be wider and larger, and more sophisticated, and unfortunately more effective, the only best plan for an internet infrastructure to stay safe from it is to prepare for it with back-up solutions and be ready to involve the ISP and all its partners to overcome the challenges ahead because the question is no longer: could an attack that can cripple the internet for longer period of time happen? But rather: when? And could an organization recover from it? This scenario will be revealed in my next book:

The Internet Collapse and the Next Society.
Technological, Societal and Economical Analysis.

And also enjoy my funny to read book:

IoT Botnets: the Army of Ones and Zeros:
Your helpful devices that don't always work for you!

References

Arrow. (September 13, 2016). IoT operating systems. Retrieved from https://www.arrow.com/en/research-and-events/articles/iot-operating-systems

Ball, T. (2017). Top 5 critical infrastructure cyber-attacks. Retrieved from https://www.cbronline.com/cybersecurity/top-5-infrastructure-hacks/

Barman, S. (2002). Writing information security policies. (p, 27). Indianapolis, IN: New Riders Publishing

Convery, S. (2012). Network security architecture. (p. 98). Indianapolis, IN: Cisco Press.

Dube, R. (2009). Top 5 websites to learn how to hack like a pro. Retrieved from http://www.makeuseof.com/tag/top-5-websites-to-learn-how-to-hack-like-a-pro/

Dyn DDoS, (n. d.). Explore DDoS. Retrieved from https://dyn.com/ddos/

Dyn Internet Intelligence. (n. d.). Internet intelligence – network. Retrieved from https://dyn.com/dyn-internet-intelligence/

Dyn Managed DNS, (n. d.). DNS, DNS products trusted by world's most admired digital brands. Retrieved from https://dyn.com/dns/managed-dns/

DHS, (n. d.). Critical infrastructure sector partnerships. Retrieved from https://www.dhs.gov/critical-infrastructure-sector-partnerships

Friedman, T. (2005). The world is flat. (pp. 51-199). New York, NY: Farrar, Staus and Giroux

Green, T. (October 21, 2016). How the Dyn DDoS attack unfolded. Retrieved from https://www.networkworld.com/article/3134057/security/how-the-Dyn-ddos-attack-unfolded.html

HCR. (2016). The human capital reports. Retrieved from https://www.weforum.org/reports/the-human-capital-report-2016

Herzberg, B., Bekeman, D., and Zeifman, I. (2016). Breaking down Mirai: an IoT DDoS botnet analysis. Retrieved from https://www.incapsula.com/blog/malware-analysis-Mirai-DDoS-botnet.html

Hilton, S. (October 26, 2016). Dyn Analysis Summary of Friday October 21 Attack. Retrieved from https://dyn.com/blog/dyn-analysis-summary-of-friday-october-21-attack/

Krebs, B. (January 2017). Who is Anna-Senpai, the Mirai Worm Author? Retrieved from https://krebsonsecurity.com/2017/01/who-is-anna-senpai-the-mirai-worm-author/

Liu, Y. (December 9, 2016). Linux.Gafgyt. Retrieved from https://www.symantec.com/security_response/writeup.jsp?docid=2014-100222-5658-99&tabid=2

Mark, G., Czerwinski, M., Bell, G., Pea, R., Dey, A., Soojung-Kim, A., and Mazmanian, M. (2016). Constantly connected: At what price and with what rewards? In Proceedings of the 19th ACM Conference on Computer Supported Cooperative Work and Social Computing Companion (CSCW '16 Companion). ACM, New York, NY, USA, 204-209. Retrieved from https://doi-org.ufairfax.idm.oclc.org/10.1145/2818052.2893364

Mohan, R. (2010). Anycast – three reasons why your DNS network should use it. Retrieved from http://www.securityweek.com/content/anycast-three-reasons-why-your-dns-network-should-use-it

Nguyen, C and Goldman, J.,. (2010). Malware analysis reverse engineering (MARE) methodology & malware defense (M.D.) timeline. In *2010 Information Security Curriculum Development Conference* (InfoSecCD '10). ACM, New York, NY, USA, 8-14. Retrieved from http://dx.doi.org.ufairfax.idm.oclc.org/10.1145/1940941.

1940944

NIST (February, 2014). Framework for improving critical infrastructure cybersecurity. (p. 1). Retrieved from https://www.nist.gov/sites/default/files/documents/cyber framework/cybersecurity-framework-021214.pdf

Nixon, C., Costello, E., and Wikholm, Z. (October 25, 2016). An after-action analysis of the Mirai botnet attacks on Dyn. Retrieved from https://www.flashpoint-intel.com/blog/cybercrime/action-analysis-mirai-botnet-attacks-dyn/

Schneier, B. (November 1, 2016). Lessons from the Dyn DDoS Attack. Retrieved from https://securityintelligence.com/lessons-from-the-dyn-ddos-attack/

Schudel, G. (n. d.). Bandwidth, Packets Per Second, and Other Network Performance Metrics. Retrieved from https://www.cisco.com/c/en/us/about/security-center/network-performance-metrics.html

Statista.com. (2017). Daily time spent on social networking by internet users worldwide from 2012 to 2017 (in minutes). Retrieved from https://www.statista.com/statistics/433871/daily-social-media-usage-worldwide/

Steadman, M. (2016). DDoS Mitigation: Inside Dyn's Internet Performance Management Approach. Retrieved from https://dyn.com/blog/ddos-mitigation-inside-dyns-internet-performance-management-approach/

Thakar, B. and Parekh, C., (2016). Advance Persistent Threat: Botnet. In *Proceedings of the Second International Conference on Information and Communication Technology for Competitive Strategies* (ICTCS '16). ACM, New York, NY, USA, , Article 143. Page 5. Retrieved from http://dx.doi.org.ufairfax.idm.oclc.org/10.1145/2905055.2905360

US-CERT Bulletin SB16-298. (October 24, 2016).
Vulnerability Summary for the Week of October 17,
2016. Retrieved from https://www.us-
cert.gov/ncas/bulletins/SB16-298

US-CERT DDoS (2014). Quick guide mitigation. Retrieved
from https://www.us-
cert.gov/sites/default/files/publications/DDoS%20Quick
%20Guide.pdf

US-CERT Security Tip ST05-017. (October 25, 2016).
Cybersecurity for electronic devices. Retrieved
from https://www.us-cert.gov/ncas/tips/ST05-017

US-CERT Vulnerability Note VU#243144. (October 21,
2016). Vulnerability note VU#243144 Linux kernel
memory subsystem copy on write mechanism
contains a race condition vulnerability. Retrieved
from https://www.kb.cert.org/vuls/id/243144

US-CERT Week 3, (October 17, 2016). Week three of
national cybersecurity awareness month. Retrieved
from https://www.us-cert.gov/ncas/current-
activity/2016/10/17/Week-Three-National-Cyber-
Security-Awareness-Month

Weissman, C. (2015). Some hackers make more than
$80,000 a month - here's how. Retrieved from
http://www.businessinsider.com/we-found-out-how-
much-money-hackers-actually-make-2015-7/#rums--the-
online-places-where-cybercriminals-sell-their-goods-1

WHO Statistics. (2009). Demographic and socioeconomic
statistics. Retrieved from
http://www.who.int/whosis/whostat/EN_WHS09_T
able9.pdf

Why Dyn, (n.d.). Customer success stories. Retrieved from
https://dyn.com/success-stories/

Willige, A. (2017). The state of the world in 2016 – in
charts. Retrieved from
https://www.weforum.org/agenda/2017/01/state-of-
the-world-in-2016-in-charts/

World Bank Group. (2017). The little data book on

information and communication technology.
Retrieved from
https://openknowledge.worldbank.org/bitstream/handle/
10986/25737/9781464810282.pdf

World Development Indicators. (2016). World
development indicators: the information society.
Retrieved from http://wdi.worldbank.org/table/5.12

York, K. (October 22, 2016). Dyn Statement on 10/21/2016
DDoS Attack. Retrieved from
https://dyn.com/blog/dyn-statement-on-10212016-ddos-
attack/

Table of Figures

www.ingramcontent.com/pod-product-compliance
Lightning Source LLC
Chambersburg PA
CBHW041153050326
40690CB00001B/461